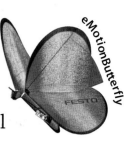
eMotionButterfly
FESTO

SwagBot

Dot

Pleurobot

Marty

Wakamaru

What is a robot?

Robots are machines that can do many amazing things. They build cars, explore space, and fix our bodies. Like humans, a robot needs to see, hear, or feel with its senses, and move its body. Robots, just like us, also need energy to work and intelligence to make decisions.

HRP-3 Promet MK-II

Energy

Moving, sensing, and thinking all need energy. Robots usually run on electricity. They get this electricity either from being plugged into a power supply or from batteries, like Promet MK-II's battery backpack.

Sensing

Robots use sensors to see, hear, and feel. The Mars rover *Curiosity* has cameras for eyes to see where it is going. Some robots have senses that we don't have, such as being able to see heat.

Curiosity

Timeline of robotics

Below you'll see some of the first robots ever invented, and how they get more advanced as the timeline gets closer to the present.

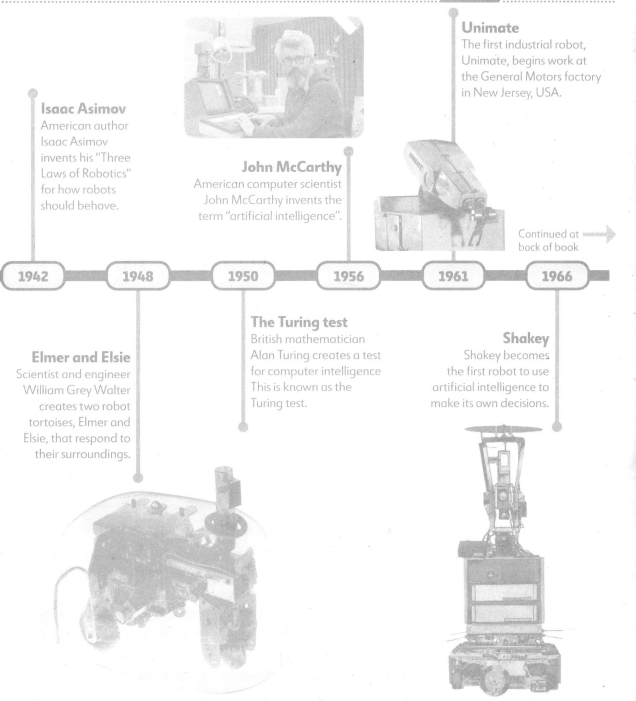

Unimate
The first industrial robot, Unimate, begins work at the General Motors factory in New Jersey, USA.

Isaac Asimov
American author Isaac Asimov invents his "Three Laws of Robotics" for how robots should behave.

John McCarthy
American computer scientist John McCarthy invents the term "artificial intelligence".

Continued at back of book

| 1942 | 1948 | 1950 | 1956 | 1961 | 1966 |

The Turing test
British mathematician Alan Turing creates a test for computer intelligence This is known as the Turing test.

Shakey
Shakey becomes the first robot to use artificial intelligence to make its own decisions.

Elmer and Elsie
Scientist and engineer William Grey Walter creates two robot tortoises, Elmer and Elsie, that respond to their surroundings.

Things to find out:

DK findout!

Robots

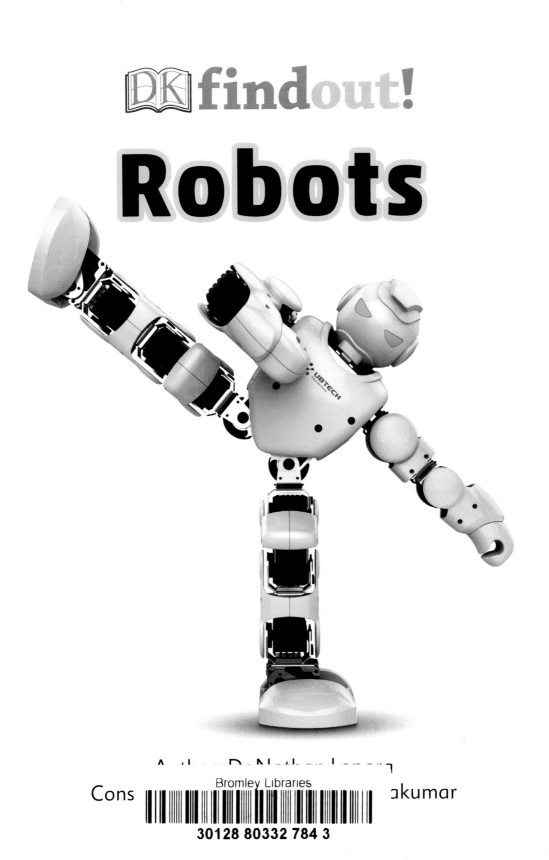

Author: Dr Nathan Lepora

Editors Olivia Stanford, Kritika Gupta
Project art editor Hoa Luc
Art editor Radhika Banerjee
Assistant art editor Shubham Rohatgi
Senior DTP designer Neeraj Bhatia
DTP designer Dheeraj Singh
Picture researcher Aditya Katyal
Jacket co-ordinator Francesca Young
Jacket designers Amy Keast, Suzena Sengupta
Managing editors Laura Gilbert,
Monica Saigal
Managing art editor Diane Peyton Jones
Deputy managing art editor Ivy Sengupta
Pre-production producer Nadine King
Producer Isabell Schart
Art director Martin Wilson
Publisher Sarah Larter
Publishing director Sophie Mitchell

Educational consultant Jacqueline Harris

First published in Great Britain in 2018 by
Dorling Kindersley Limited
80 Strand, London, WC2R 0RL

Copyright © 2018 Dorling Kindersley Limited
A Penguin Random House Company
10 9 8 7 6 5 4 3 2 1
001–307838–Jan/2018

A CIP catalogue record for this book
is available from the British Library.
ISBN: 978-0-2413-1589-7

Printed and bound in China

A WORLD OF IDEAS:
SEE ALL THERE IS TO KNOW

www.dk.com

Contents

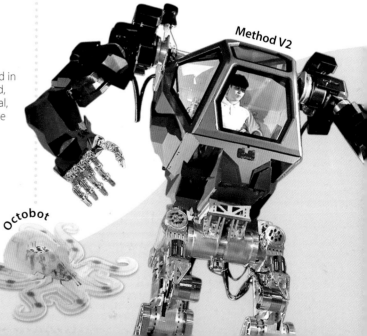

Method V2

Octobot

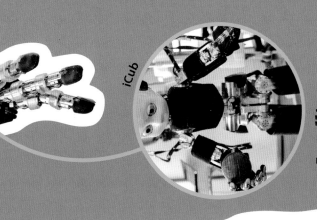

iCub

Intelligence

Robots need intelligence to decide what to do. Most robots use computers as their "brains". Modern robots, such as iCub, can learn from their surroundings.

There are some jobs that robots are much better at than people. The four main reasons we use robots to do something are because a job is:

1 Dangerous Places or tasks that would harm people.

2 Dull Long and repetitive tasks that are boring.

3 Dirty In unpleasant places like sewers and mines.

4 Delicate Too difficult to do with our hands.

Romeo

Movement

Inside a robot are motors to move the parts of its body. Most robots move around on wheels. Others, such as Romeo, have legs.

Early robots

Inventors have designed robots since ancient times. Before modern robots there were automata – moving machines driven by clockwork, air, or water. In the 20th century, robots began to run on electricity and use computers to think for themselves.

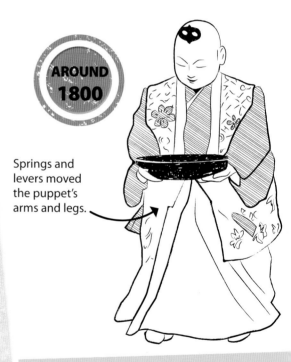

AROUND 1800

Springs and levers moved the puppet's arms and legs.

The water that drove the clock was hidden inside the elephant's body.

The elephant clock

This automaton was designed by al-Jazari, an Arab inventor. The clock was driven by water, which caused the man to strike a cymbal and the bird to whistle every half an hour.

Karakuri puppets

These mechanical dolls from Japan could act out stories for the theatre or even serve tea to guests! Karakuri is a Japanese word meaning "trick" or "mechanisms".

Eric

1928

Eric was a human-shaped automaton that was 2 m (7 ft) tall. Inside its body were kilometres of wires connected to motors. These made it stand and sit down, turn to the left and right, and wave its arms while talking.

Eric's armour made it look like a knight.

1948

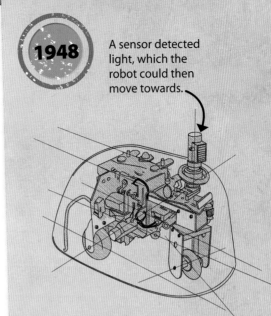

A sensor detected light, which the robot could then move towards.

Elmer and Elsie

These tortoise-like machines were the first robots to make their own decisions. Scientist William Grey Walter designed them to react to their surroundings like real animals.

Shakey

1966

Shakey was the first robot able to think for itself. From looking around a room with a camera, it could plan how to move around without bumping into things.

Shakey was connected to its computer "brain" by radio.

7

Famous robot engineers

There has been huge progress in robotics over the last 50 years. Robots have changed from large, clunky machines into sleek, lifelike devices. Thousands of scientists and engineers have helped develop the fantastic robots we have today. Here are a few of the most famous.

! WOW!

Over **500 years** ago, the famous artist **Leonardo da Vinci** designed a humanoid knight!

HIROSHI ISHIGURO

Hiroshi Ishiguro is a Japanese engineer who builds robots that look like real people. He calls these robots "Geminoids™". His laboratory has built a Geminoid™ of himself and of several other people.

Hiroshi Ishiguro and his Geminoid™
Geminoid™ HI-4: Osaka University

RODNEY BROOKS

Australian engineer Rodney Brooks is famous both as a scientist and a businessman. He built a famous humanoid robot called Cog that learns like a human. He also started the companies that make the robot vacuum cleaner Roomba and the worker robot Baxter.

Rodney Brooks with Cog

CYNTHIA BREAZEAL

Cynthia Breazeal is an American engineer who makes social robots that people can talk to and play with. Her robots often have faces that show feelings such as happiness, sadness, or fear.

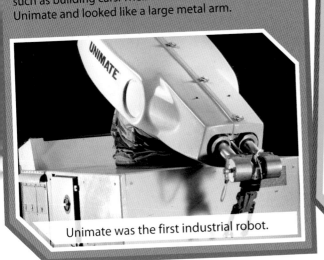

Leonardo is a fluffy social robot.

SEBASTIAN THRUN

German Sebastian Thrun and a team of engineers built a self-driving car called Stanley. In 2005, Stanley won a tricky, self-driving car race called the DARPA Grand Challenge, which includes racing round mountains.

Stanley is a robot car that drives itself.

JOSEPH F. ENGELBERGER

American Joseph F. Engelberger and his colleague George Devol made the first industrial robot. These robots work in factories and do jobs such as building cars. Their robot was called Unimate and looked like a large metal arm.

Unimate was the first industrial robot.

RUZENA BAJCSY

Ruzena Bajcsy is an American engineer who invents ways for robots to sense the world like humans. She worked on robot hands that feel and eyes that look around. Her laboratory can also scan your body to store your movements inside a computer.

A person's moves are stored in a computer.

North America

Atlas is made in the USA and is one of the world's best robots at walking and balancing. It is designed to travel over difficult ground and if it trips, it can stop itself falling over. One day it could help rescue people.

Atlas

Atlas Robot image courtesy of Boston Dynamics.

By **2025** Japan expects to have **1 million** industrial robots.

Wheelie moves when you move your face

Key Expression: FULLSMILE

Robots around the world

Wheelie

Amazing robots are being built all around the world. From agricultural robots that patrol Australia's huge farms to nursing robots that help care for Japan's ageing population, new types of robot can help in many different ways. The designs for these robots can be shared around the globe.

South America

Wheelie is a robot wheelchair developed in Brazil by HOOBOX Robotics. This chair is for people who cannot walk or move their hands. You can tell Wheelie where to go by speaking or pulling different faces.

Europe

YuMi is a two-armed robot created for working in factories. It can work with humans without accidentally harming them and can even make paper aeroplanes.

YuMi

Asia

ROBEAR is a Japanese nursing robot that looks like a friendly bear. It weighs 140 kg (309 lb) and has padded arms. It can gently lift a sick patient into a bed or wheelchair.

ROBEAR

YuMi helping to make plug sockets

ROBEAR helps a woman into a wheelchair

Traffic robot

SwagBot

Africa

These giant robot police officers direct traffic in Kinshasa, Democratic Republic of the Congo. Standing 2.5 m (8 ft) high, they also tell people when to cross the road.

SwagBot patrolling a field

Australasia

SwagBot is a robot cowboy from Australia that helps farmers. The robot is designed to drive around huge areas of land, watching cows and helping to herd them around.

Types of robot

Do you need help with something? This quiz will help you find out which robot you need. Robots are grouped together by the jobs that they do. Their most common work is in homes and factories. However, they can do much more – even exploring space!

Industrial

Some robots make things such as cars and televisions – like Baxter, a factory robot. Go to page 15 to find out why this robot is also called a cobot.

Baxter

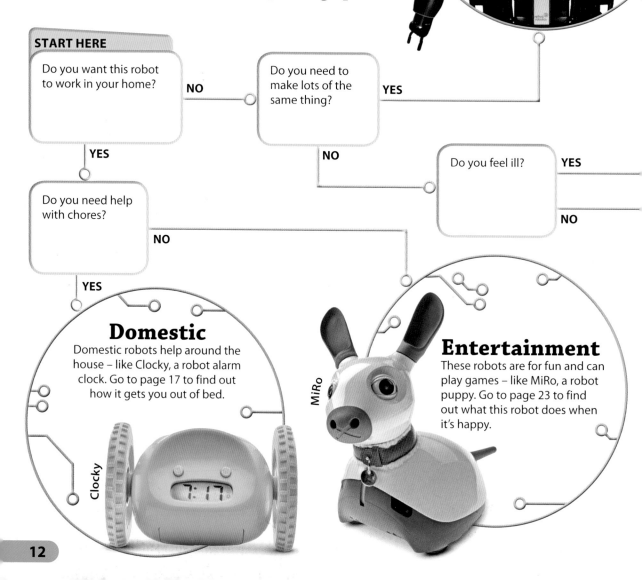

START HERE

Do you want this robot to work in your home?

NO

Do you need to make lots of the same thing?

YES

YES

Do you need help with chores?

NO

Do you feel ill?

YES

NO

NO

YES

Domestic

Domestic robots help around the house – like Clocky, a robot alarm clock. Go to page 17 to find out how it gets you out of bed.

Clocky

7:17

MiRo

Entertainment

These robots are for fun and can play games – like MiRo, a robot puppy. Go to page 23 to find out what this robot does when it's happy.

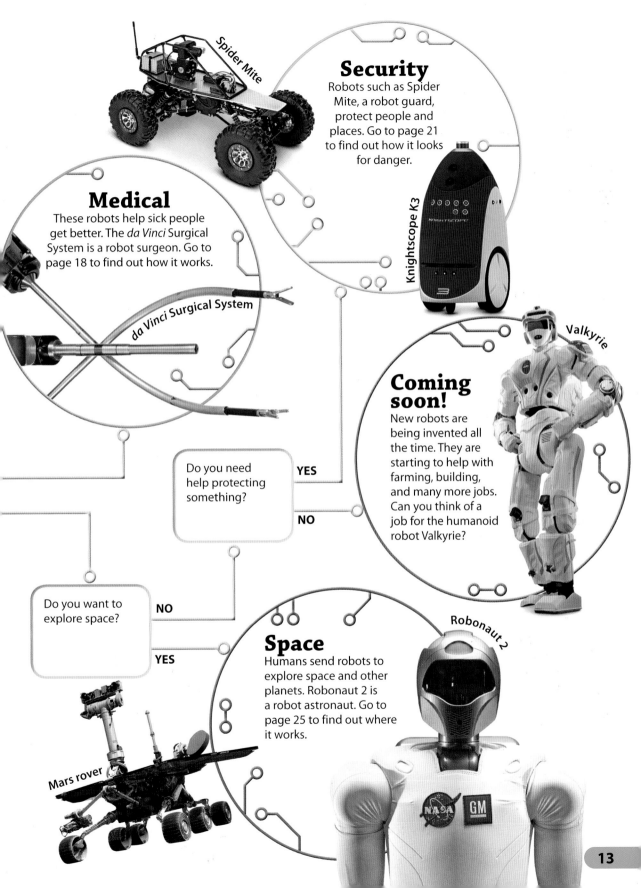

Spider Mite

Security

Robots such as Spider Mite, a robot guard, protect people and places. Go to page 21 to find out how it looks for danger.

Knightscope K3

Medical

These robots help sick people get better. The *da Vinci* Surgical System is a robot surgeon. Go to page 18 to find out how it works.

da Vinci Surgical System

Valkyrie

Coming soon!

New robots are being invented all the time. They are starting to help with farming, building, and many more jobs. Can you think of a job for the humanoid robot Valkyrie?

Do you need help protecting something?

YES

NO

Do you want to explore space?

NO

YES

Robonaut 2

Space

Humans send robots to explore space and other planets. Robonaut 2 is a robot astronaut. Go to page 25 to find out where it works.

Mars rover

NASA   GM

At the end of the arm is a gripper that can hold objects.

REALLY?

!

Robotic arms are so precise that they can place items to within the width of a **single hair!**

Robots at work

Groups of companies that make certain products, such as cars, in factories are called industries. They use teams of industrial robots to pick up heavy objects, paint in different colours, and put together parts, all without getting tired or bored.

Robotic arms The most common type of industrial robot is shaped like an arm. The KR 1000 Titan is a huge arm that can lift up to 1,300 kg (2,870 lb). That's the weight of an adult rhinoceros!

Inside the arm are powerful electric motors.

Cobots

There are now new types of industrial robot helpers, called cobots. They can work safely alongside people in factories. Baxter is a cobot that can be trained by a co-worker. A person just has to move Baxter's arms to show it how to do something.

A Baxter robot packs boxes in a factory.

Robots at home

Mini-drones can be used to carry small items around. The Parrot Mambo can carry objects weighing up to 4 g (0.14 oz).

Imagine having a robot that could tidy your bedroom, put out the bins, and cook your food! These chores around the home are jobs for home or "domestic" robots. Domestic robots of the future will be able to do more and more of the boring jobs that people do now.

Buddy

This cute family robot can learn to recognize people and play games. It even knows hide-and-seek!

WOW!

Over **15 million** Roombas have been made – enough for almost everyone in **London** and **New York City**.

Roomba

Millions of homes use this robot vacuum cleaner to keep floors dirt-free. It uses sensors to avoid objects in its way.

Clocky

Clocky is a robot alarm clock. It runs away from you so you have to get out of bed to turn it off!

The FoldiMate folds clean clothes.

Robotic Kitchen

Scientists are working on a two-armed "robo chef". One day it could chop, mix, and cook to make meals from a library of recipes.

Braava 380t is a robotic mop that cleans the floor.

L30 Elite

This wheeled robot moves up and down your garden to neatly trim the grass. It goes back to its base if it starts raining.

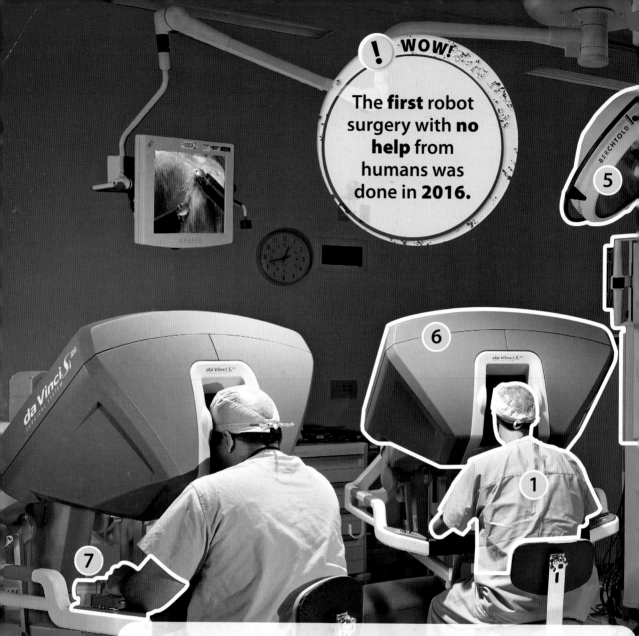

The **first** robot surgery with **no help** from humans was done in **2016**.

Medical robots

Robots can be used in hospitals to help treat sick and injured people. Doctors even use robots for operations. Using the *da Vinci* Surgical System, surgeons control robot arms so they can operate on tiny areas of the body.

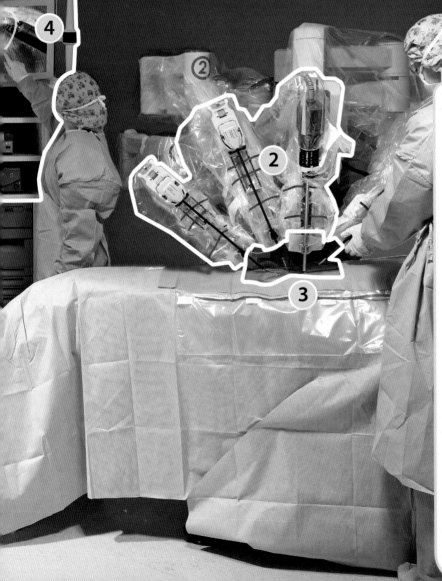

WHAT'S IN THE PICTURE?

1   **Surgeon** Human surgeons are in control of the robot's movements.

2   **Robot arms** Four arms hold the surgical tools for operating on the patient.

3   **Surgical tools** The arms hold tiny scissors, scalpels, and other tools.

4   **Monitor** The monitor is connected to a camera in a tube so the doctors can see inside the patient.

5   **Surgical light** These lights help the team see the operating area.

6   **Console** The surgeons sit at a console that contains the controls and a close-up view of the operating area.

7   **Joysticks** The surgeons move these joysticks to control the robot arms and tools.

Security robots

Robots make great security guards. They can wait silently for a long time and when they see something unusual, they call the police or sound an alarm. Some security robots have arms that can be used to pick up suspicious items. They can also be remote-controlled, so people can stay at a safe distance.

GUARDROBO D1

This robot guards against intruders, fires, and leaks. It even carries a fire extinguisher to put out fires.

TALON

Talon is a robot used in the army to find bombs and land mines, and make them safe. Its arm and gripper can be controlled by a remote to pick up objects.

BigDog

BigDog is a four-legged robot that can carry supplies and food – like a packhorse. It can walk on stony ground, muddy trails, and even on ice!

BigDog robot image courtesy of Boston Dynamics

The camera is safe inside a frame.

SPIDER MITE

Spider Mite is like a tough, remote-controlled car. This robot can climb steep slopes and it has a camera so you can see what is happening around it. It can even see in the dark. It can be used to patrol buildings.

Big tyres help Spider Mite drive over rough ground.

Knightscope K3

Knightscope K3 patrols around shopping malls on the look-out for thieves. Its mission is to stop crime. Upon seeing anything suspicious, it alerts the police. Knightscope can also sound a loud alarm to alert people to danger.

GhostSwimmer

GhostSwimmer is designed to look like a tuna or shark. It even swims like a real fish by waggling its tail. It can dive down to 91 m (300 ft) to see what is below the surface of the water!

Fun with robots

Some robots are made to entertain us. There are many different types of entertainment robot: the smallest are robot toys and pets; the largest are robot dinosaurs in theme parks; and the loudest are robot rock bands – like Compressorhead!

Robotic pets

Robot pets are shaped like animals and are designed to play with humans. These clever robots respond to what you say and can perform tricks. You don't have to clean up after them either!

AIBO
This robot pet looks and acts like a small dog. It can learn its name and even play football!

AIBO fetches plastic bones.

Stickboy
Stickboy is a robot drummer with four arms and two legs. It has spikes for hair and moves its head in time to the music.

MiRo wags its tail when it's happy.

Compressorhead
Compressorhead are a rock band of robots. Made in Germany, there are three main members: a guitarist, a bassist, and a drummer. They may be machines but they play real instruments!

MiRo
This cute robot looks as though it is part-rabbit and part-puppy. Like an animal, it reacts to sounds and movement.

Robots in space

Space is a dangerous place for people. There is harmful radiation, no air to breathe, and it takes a very long time to get anywhere! Scientists have built many robots to help us explore it. Some robot craft circle alien planets, but others have landed to take a close-up look.

Cassini

This spacecraft was sent to explore the planet Saturn, its moons, and rings. It took nearly seven years to get there.

Voyager I

This robot has travelled for around 40 years and is now outside the Solar System. It is the first robot to reach interstellar space.

Space snaps

Space exploration robots have cameras to take photographs. As well as lots of scientific information, these robots send photos back to Earth. These show amazing sights never seen before by people.

Curiosity photographed this hill on Mars. The colour has been changed so the scene appears how it would look on Earth.

International Space
Station (ISS)

Mars rovers

Three of these wheeled
robots are on the surface of
Mars – *Opportunity*, *Spirit*,
and *Curiosity*. Two continue
to study the planet's surface.

Robonaut 2

Robonaut 2 is a robot
astronaut. It works on the
ISS, where it helps human
astronauts with jobs such
as repairs.

Rosetta

This spacecraft filmed,
and then crashed into,
a comet – a ball of rock
and ice far out in space.

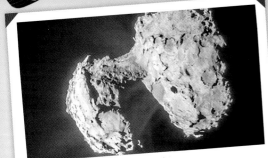

Rosetta photographed the comet
67P/Churyumov-Gerasimenko in 2015.

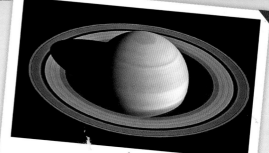

Cassini took this photo of Saturn
and its rings in 2016.

A day with robots

There are more and more robots around us in the world. They can help at home, at work, drive us around, carry our shopping, make deliveries, and be our friends. Let us imagine a day in the future with your robot helpers.

Waymo

You start the day by getting in a robot car such as Waymo. However, you don't need to touch the steering wheel. It can sense other cars and people, to drive you safely to work.

Waymo, take me to work!

Aiko Chihira

When you arrive at your office, you are greeted by a robot receptionist. Aiko can speak, and knows sign language.

Hello! Have a nice day.

That's a great idea!

BeamPro telepresence robot

You have a meeting, but it's at another office. No problem, your telepresence robot is there. You can use it to look around, and it has a screen attached so you can see and talk through it.

Gita

After work it is time to go shopping. Gita, your robot porter, carries your groceries for you. While you walk around, it rolls after you.

ROLLING, ROLLING, ROLLING.

Delivery robot

You get home and realize you've forgotten to buy something! That's OK. A delivery robot will collect your shopping, then drive it to your house to drop it off.

Just in time.

Marty

You would like to learn more about robots, so you make one yourself! Marty is a walking robot that you build from a kit. It can be programmed to carry out simple tasks, such as dancing.

Great moves Marty!

Wakamaru

When you walk through the door you are greeted by your friendly home robot, Wakamaru. It offers to read out your emails while you sit down and relax.

Welcome back!

Building a robot

Complex robots can have millions of different parts. Most are built in factories. Some industrial robots are even built using finished copies of themselves! A technology called "3D printing" is helping people build their own robots at home. The printer makes the robot parts, which you can then assemble.

These wires allow Poppy to be plugged in to a power supply.

This microchip is part of the robot's computer brain.

3D printing

Regular printing puts images on flat objects such as sheets of paper – just like in a book. 3D printers make three dimensional (3D) solid objects, which have height, length, and width. To do this, most printers squeeze plastic out of a tube, in the same way you would put icing on a cake!

These bags contain the screws and wires used to connect the robot's electronics and body parts.

A 3D printer making a plastic model

Plenty of parts
In order to build a robot, you need body parts that will give the robot shape, motors to make it move, microchips so it can think, and lots of wires and screws to connect it all together! Here are the pieces for a Poppy robot.

The robot's body parts are made using a 3D printer.

A plastic head will contain the computer brain.

Poppy complete

Poppy is a humanoid robot that stands 83 cm (33 in) tall. Its body parts are made on a 3D printer. These parts are joined to 25 motors to make Poppy move. The finished Poppy can walk and dance!

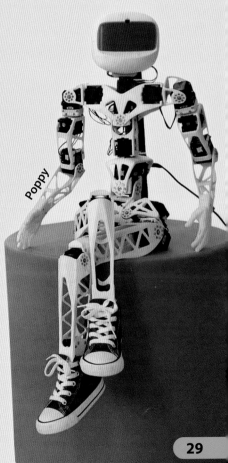

Poppy

This model has hands that are fixed, so the robot can't pick up small objects.

Lots of different body parts allow the robot to bend at its joints, just like a human skeleton!

These are the motors that allow the robot to move. They are also called actuators.

Feet make sure that Poppy can stand up without falling over.

Coding a robot

Robots use computer code to tell them what to do. Code is made up of lines of instructions that can be written in different "languages". Robots read these instructions in order – like when you read how to build a model. Follow the code on this page to see how the robot works.

The robot is built to look like a penguin.

A computer inside the robot receives instructions from a phone or tablet.

UBTECH

! WOW!

The code that runs Google is **two billion lines long!**

Coding with blocks

This programming language uses coloured blocks to tell the robot what to do. If the robot reads code words such as "if" or "else", it knows to check for something to happen – such as you tilting your phone to the left. This makes it "do" an action, such as dancing or walking.

If the phone or tablet is tilted left the penguin moves left.

If the phone or tablet isn't tilted left the penguin dances happily.

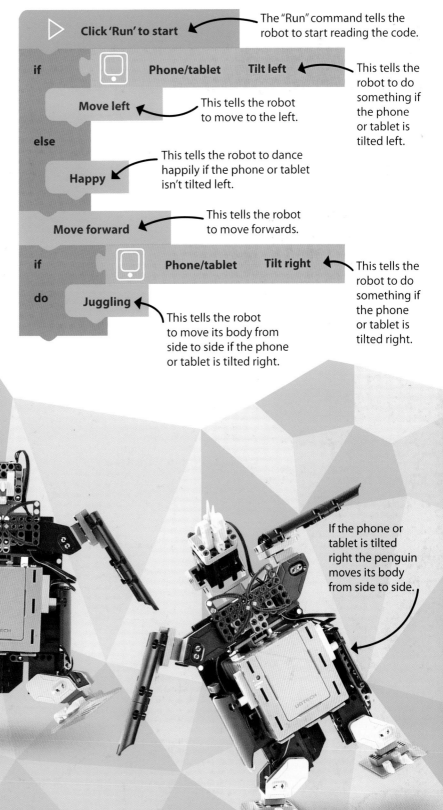

The "Run" command tells the robot to start reading the code.

Click 'Run' to start

if   Phone/tablet   Tilt left

This tells the robot to do something if the phone or tablet is tilted left.

Move left

This tells the robot to move to the left.

else

Happy

This tells the robot to dance happily if the phone or tablet isn't tilted left.

Move forward

This tells the robot to move forwards.

if   Phone/tablet   Tilt right

This tells the robot to do something if the phone or tablet is tilted right.

do   Juggling

This tells the robot to move its body from side to side if the phone or tablet is tilted right.

If the phone or tablet is tilted right the penguin moves its body from side to side.

Swarm robots

Robot swarms are made from large groups of simple robots teaming up. The whole swarm works together to function as one bigger, more intelligent robot. Robot swarms can do things that would be difficult for other robots to do, such as changing shape.

Swarm intelligence

Swarm robots must send messages to each other to know what to do. To make a "K" shape, these robots communicate with those nearest them to find out if they are in the right place.

Copying nature

Animals like ants form swarms to do things they could not do alone, for example, moving big objects. Robots such as BionicANTs that imitate the behaviour of animals are called "biomimetic" robots because they copy, or mimic, nature.

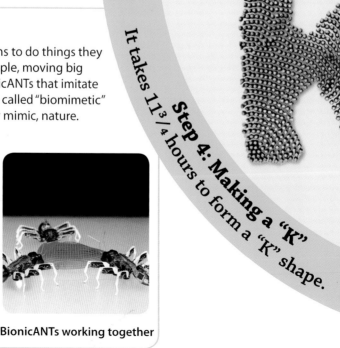

Step 1: Random group
The robots start clustered together in a random shape.

Step 4: Making a "K"
It takes 11³/₄ hours to form a "K" shape.

Ants working together   BionicANTs working together

Step 2: Beginning to move
Four "seed" robots tell the group where to start.

Step 3: Taking shape
The robots move around the edge until they find a free space.

Kilobots

The "K" swarm is made of over 1,000 individuals, called kilobots. Each one is coin-sized, with three thin legs, and moves by vibrating. Kilobots use infrared light to send messages to each other.

33

Drones

Flying robots are called drones. Some look like miniature aeroplanes and others like helicopters with lots of blades. The largest drones are as big as jet aircraft, but the smallest are tiny fliers about 3 cm (1 in) across. Most carry cameras to show people their view from the air.

How drones work

Drones can be remote-controlled or fly themselves. Both types use spinning blades to keep them up in the air. The best drones are clever enough to fly straight even when it's windy.

Flying high
This drone, also called a quadcopter, has four helicopter blades. Each blade spins like a fan. These push air down to lift the robot up.

Spinning blade

Spinning blade

Lift

Lift

Phantom 3

Camera

Remote control
Controls on a remote let the user tell the robot where to move. A tablet screen shows the view from the robot's camera so you can get the perfect shot.

Eye in the sky This photograph was taken by a drone flying above the boat. Drones can take amazing photos that would be almost impossible to capture otherwise – like this one of a humpback whale!

Robot explorers

There are places on Earth that are difficult for people to visit. The bottom of the sea, the icy polar regions, and inside volcanoes are just some of these. Scientists have created robots to help us see these exciting places.

Crabster CR200
How would you like to meet a crab that is 1.3 m (4 ft) tall? Crabster walks along the seafloor, where the tide is too strong for divers.

Solar panels generate electricity for energy.

GROVER
Explorers built this robot to work in the coldest temperatures on Earth. It it designed to drive over frozen ice sheets in the Arctic.

Each leg has multiple joints that bend.

OceanOne
This underwater robot has a human-shaped body, but propellers instead of legs. Scientists used it to find treasure on a shipwreck 100 m (328 ft) deep!

OceanOne's hands let its controller feel what the robot is touching.

VolcanoBot 1

Scientists built this small two-wheeled robot to explore vents in volcanoes where lava has escaped. It is only 30 cm (1 ft) long.

VolcanoBot 1 can fit into small cracks.

Nomad

This four-wheeled robot is the size of a small car. Nomad can explore dry places such as deserts, which are similar to the surface of planets like Mars.

pecial tyres help
Iomad roll
cross sand.

Pyramid Rover

Inside the Great Pyramid of Giza, in Egypt, is a tunnel that is too narrow for a person. Scientists built Pyramid Rover to explore the tunnel. At the end of the tunnel it drilled a hole through a stone door and discovered a secret room with a second door. No one knows what, if anything, lies beyond the next door!

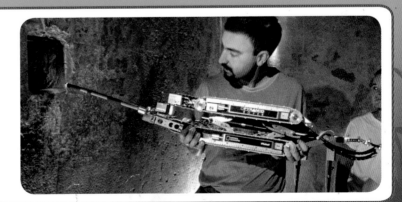

Pleurobot

Scientists designed this robot to look and move like a salamander – a slimy, lizard-like amphibian. On land, it walks on four legs. In water, it swims by wriggling its body from side to side.

Animal robots

Animals are able to do extraordinary things. Kangaroos bound for miles across deserts, lizards grip onto vertical walls, and bees zoom through the air. Scientists make robots that copy animals, to learn how animals do these things and so that machines can do them too.

Robotic Fish

Robotic Fish

Just like an actual fish, these swimming robots have lifelike skin covered in scales. When people see them in a tank, they can mistake them for real fish because they swim so well.

Pleurobot

Stickybot

Stickybot is a robot lizard that can climb up walls. Its feet have a special sticky skin, like that of a gecko lizard. Tiny hairs on its toes can stick to almost any surface.

Stickybot

eMotionButterflies

These flying robots look like giant, flapping butterflies. Their wings are 50 cm (20 in) across, making them about 10 times the size of a garden butterfly.

eMotionButterfly

BionicKangaroo

BionicKangaroo is shaped like a small kangaroo. It can hop the length of its body without falling over – about 1 m (3 ft).

BionicKangaroo

FESTO

RoboBees

These tiny robots can fly like bees. They are so lifelike that their wings make buzzing sounds when they fly. RoboBees could work in large groups, called swarms.

RoboBee

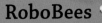

Animatronics

Animatronic models are robots made to look like living animals or people. They are mechanical puppets that are moved by motors rather than strings. Animatronics are often used in films to bring creatures like dinosaurs to life. You can also see them in many theme parks and museums.

What's inside?

Inside this animatronic dinosaur is a metal skeleton connected to motors. The motors move the different parts to make the dinosaur seem as though it is alive. As the skeleton moves, the eyes look around and the stomach moves in and out, so the dinosaur looks as if it is breathing.

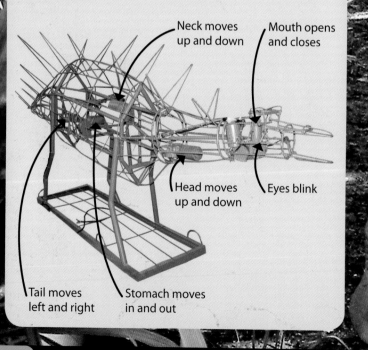

Neck moves up and down

Mouth opens and closes

Head moves up and down

Eyes blink

Tail moves left and right

Stomach moves in and out

Dynamic dinosaur This animatronic dinosaur looks like a Stegosaurus. It can move its head, mouth, eyes, stomach, hips, and tail. It is about 6 m (20 ft) long and 3 m (10 ft) high – that's about as big as an elephant!

The **T. rex** built for the film *Jurassic Park* was **12 m (39 ft) long** and **6 m (20 ft) high.**

Artists have to guess the colours to paint dinosaurs as no one knows what most dinosaurs looked like.

The finished dinosaur is covered with a lifelike skin made of a rubbery material called silicone.

Soft robotics

Scientists can now build robots out of soft, squidgy materials. These soft robots are safer and less easily broken than hard robots. Soft robots are like soft-bodied animals, such as octopuses. They could be designed to squeeze through gaps and pick up delicate objects.

Octobot

Octobot is based on an octopus with eight bendy tentacles. It is made from rubbery materials and doesn't have any hard parts. It is even controlled by chemical reactions, not electricity!

Soft circuits

The circuits that control Octobot are made of a chemical liquid, rather than wires. When the liquid touches tiny pieces of metal in Octobot's head, it turns into a gas. This gas makes the arms move.

Soft gripper

A chameleon's long tongue can grab insects instantly thanks to the tongue's flexible tip that wraps around its prey. FlexShapeGripper is a soft robot gripper that works in the same way. Its soft tip moulds around objects to hold them securely. It can even pick up more than one object at a time!

The FlexShapeGripper picking up an object

3D printing of Octobot's circuits

Octobot is made of soft parts, including a silicone body, a liquid circuit to control its movements, and stretchy actuators, which are the parts that make the arms move.

Glow in the dark

Glowing inks inside Octobot mean you can clearly see the circuits that control the robot using special lights.

Arms moving

Each of Octobot's arms has square actuators that allow it to move. When gas enters these actuators they inflate, moving the arm – like blowing air into a balloon.

Human

Our five main senses are sight, hearing, touch, taste, and smell. We also have other senses, such as balance and temperature. Our brains use these senses to understand the world.

Hearing
Inside our ears are tiny drums, which move whenever sound hits them. This movement is how we hear sound.

Sight
Light bounces off objects and into our eyes through a small hole called a pupil. Our eyes use the light to create an image in our brain.

Smell
Inside our noses are millions of tiny sensors. These sensors recognize little particles in the air as smells.

Senses

All robots need senses to tell them what is happening around them. Humans have sense organs such as eyes, whereas robots have electrical sensors such as cameras. Many robot senses are like those of humans, but they also have some superhuman powers that we do not have.

Taste
Our tongues are covered in lots of tiny sensors called taste buds. They detect tastes such as salty and sweet.

Touch
Our skin can feel things that press against it. This sense of touch is needed to help us feel and pick up objects.

Robot

Robots also need senses so they don't bump into things and can find objects. However, robots have different senses added to them depending on the job they are designed to do.

Brainpower

Both humans and robots need to make sense of the information their sensors give them. Human sensations are sent to our brains, which then tell our bodies what to do. Robots are similar, but instead of brains, robots have computers.

Nearness

Nearness is the robot sense of distance. Robots can use infrared light or lasers to scan a room in order to map the shape of everything.

PR2

RoboGasInspector

Smell

Some robots are equipped with sensors that detect smells. These robots can be used to detect gas leaks.

Kuri

Hearing

Robots use microphones for ears. They turn sounds into electricity. A computer can then work out what the sounds mean.

— Chest microphone

NEXTAGE

Sight

Robots have cameras instead of eyes. Sometimes, robots have the cameras in their chest or even in their hands so they can see what they are picking up.

Tactile Hand

Touch

Some robots have sensitive skin that feels touch. This sense can help them hold delicate objects.

MiP

Balance

Robots need a sense of balance to move. Otherwise, they would fall over. Tilt sensors tell them which way up they are.

Humanoids

A humanoid robot has a body shaped like a person. Most humanoids have a head, chest, and two arms. Some also have legs and can walk. Others roll around on wheels. Robots that have a face and look more like people are called androids.

Pepper
When you talk to Pepper, it can tell how you feel. If you are sad it can try to cheer you up by playing a song!

NAO
Nao is a little humanoid, about the size of a baby. It is an interactive robot – great at dancing and playing football.

Romeo
This robot is designed to help elderly or sick people. It can do simple tasks such as opening doors and fetching things.

pepp

Why make an android?

One day, scientists hope that androids will do any job that a person can do. By making androids look like people, they hope co-workers may feel more comfortable working with robots.

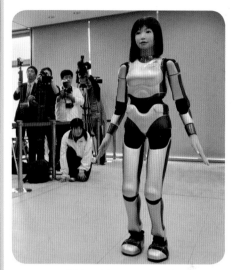

This HRP-4C android is also called Miim.

Alpha1 Pro
This little humanoid can dance, perform yoga exercises, and even do kung-fu!

RoboThespian
You can listen and watch this robot actor tell stories and jokes. It uses its hands to gesture as it speaks.

iCub
The iCub is about the height of a four-year-old child. Like a child, it needs to learn how to use its body by interacting with its environment.

What is artificial intelligence?

Artificial intelligence is a term used when machines or robots think, learn, and plan for themselves. It is commonly called "AI" for short. Computers use AI to beat people at games like chess. Self-driving cars use AI to plan how to drive along busy roads. The Internet can also work using AI, to give you the right answers in search engines.

Teaching robots

Some intelligent robots can be taught what to do. Like people, they learn from trying a task. As they repeat the task, such as when learning to tell the difference between two types of object, they get better.

The robot is also shown lots of pictures of oranges. It could be shown hundreds or even thousands of photographs.

Buddy

☑ APPLE

☑ ORANGE

The robot is shown lots of pictures of apples that it needs to remember. It is told that these are apples.

The Turing test

How do you know if a machine is as intelligent as a person? In 1950, computer scientist Alan Turing invented a clever test. A judge talks with a machine that they cannot see using text messages. If the machine can trick the judge into thinking it is a real person, it passes the test!

Alan Turing

The robot is shown a picture it has never seen before. Is it an apple or an orange?

The robot compares the new picture with its memory of the pictures it has seen before to guess what the right answer is.

APPLE

?

Pepper

Kuri

49

Superhumans

Robot technologies can help us become superhuman! Scientists have made machines that are like parts of the body. Some of these, called prosthetics, replace body parts that have been lost through injury, such as a hand or leg. Others can make us faster or stronger.

This powerful device replaces a human foot. It has a special ankle that is similar to a human ankle, helping you to walk, run, and jump.

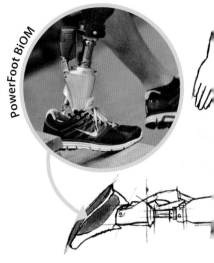

PowerFoot BiOM

Walking Assist

Argus II glasses

These special glasses can help people with damaged sight. A camera connects to a chip inside your eye and sends small electrical signals to the brain so you can see.

This robotic device superpowers your leg muscles. You wear it on your hips and thighs to walk and run faster. It is especially useful for people with weakened legs.

LUKE arm

This device replaces a human arm. It has a hand that can pick up delicate objects, such as light bulbs, and is controlled by tiny muscle movements.

HAL-5 exoskeleton

An exoskeleton is a skeleton on the outside of the body. You wear it to make you stronger, so you can lift heavy objects.

Robot friends

Social robots are designed to interact with humans. They try to understand how we feel and act, and what we say, and then respond. They can be used for everything from caring to friendship, and often have friendly faces that make us want to like them!

PARO responds when you stroke it. It is charged through a wire that connects to its mouth.

Kuri the helper robot answers a question by beeping.

Caring

PARO is a robot that looks like a baby seal. It is designed to calm patients who feel scared. It has a friendly face and cuddly body that reacts to being held. It is meant to give comfort, like a pet cat or dog.

Teaching

Kuri is a friendly, wheeled robot that helps around the home. It can follow you around and answer questions with beeps. It can even wake you up with an alarm in the morning or tell you a bedtime story at night.

The Three Laws of Robotics are rules for how robots should act around people. They were invented by author Isaac Asimov for his *Robot* series of books. The laws were invented in 1942, but are still used today. They say that a robot should:

1 Not harm humans, or let them be hurt by not helping them.

2 Obey orders from humans unless the orders break the first law.

3 Protect itself from harm unless its actions would break the first and second laws.

You can raise your hand in class using NAO even if you're at home!

Pepper can give you a hug.

Learning

NAO is a small humanoid that can be used as a telepresence robot. If you can't travel to school, it can be there for you. Using a camera and a speaker, you can talk and communicate with your class through it.

Friendship

Pepper is a companion robot who can recognize your emotions. It uses your face and voice to work out how you are, and changes its behaviour according to how you feel.

Maja with the robots Maki, and Spritebot in its green "Kiwi" skin.

Interview with...

We put some questions to Dr Maja Matarić, a professor at the University of Southern California. She runs the Interaction Lab, which develops socially assistive robots that help people.

Q: We know it is something to do with robots, but what do you actually do?

A: My students and I create robots that help people as friends and companions. For example, we created a robot that helps children in hospital cope with fear and anxiety, and a robot that recognizes bullying gestures and calls them out to help children stop being bullied or being bullies.

Q: What made you decide to become a robot engineer?

A: When I was in high school, my uncle told me computers were the future, and he was right. I wanted to make computers interact in the real, physical world – our world – and that led me to robotics.

Q: What is a usual work day for you?

A: There is no usual day! I meet with students and other scientists to invent new robots. I advise companies, show children why robotics is exciting,

Spritebot in its red "Chili" skin

go to conferences, give talks, and read and write research papers. Most of all, I work with people.

Q: What are your office and lab like?

A: My office is full of books and small toy robots for inspiration. My lab is full of students of all ages, many kinds of robots – such as Spritebot and Maki – and tools for experiments. We use all sorts of things, including people trackers, LEGO, a baby highchair, and a table-sized touch tablet.

Q: What are the best and worst parts of your job?

A: The best part is swapping ideas with students and working with them on interesting challenges. The worst part is too many emails.

Q: Do you have a favourite robot?

A: WALL-E from the film is a perfect robot. It is appealing, caring, friendly, fun, but imperfect. It has the best of human qualities without the worst.

Q: How do you think robots will help us in the future?

A: Early robots were created for dirty, dull, and dangerous jobs. Now they are created for everything. I believe that robot companions are some of the most important types of robots. Everyone should have a friend that is always there for them.

Future of robotics

In the future, there will be lots of robots. They'll help us at home, at work, in hospitals, and even inside our bodies. They will also become easier to communicate with. Robots may become so lifelike that we won't even think of them as robots any more!

Personal robots

Robots in the future may help us more in everyday life and act as personal assistants. You will also be able to program them to do what you want. In the future, everyone may have their own robot helper!

Dash

Dash and Dot are robots that anyone can program.

Dot

Dash can be programmed to play tunes on a xylophone.

SAM100 the bricklaying robot

Robot builders

Future houses could be built entirely by robots. The robot bricklayer SAM100 can work six times faster than a human, placing 3,000 bricks a day. Other houses may be 3D printed using giant robotic arms.

Self-assembling furniture

Imagine your tables and chairs could change shape and move. Scientists are working on self-assembling robots that join up to make furniture. A table could change into a chair and walk across the room!

Roombots are small robots that can twist and join up to make furniture.

Guardian LF1 catches lionfish that have been introduced into the Atlantic Ocean.

Robots with feelings

Most robots today look and behave like any other machine. Future robots could feel happy or sad just like people. This would help them understand what people want and even become our friends!

Nexi can appear to show feelings, but it doesn't have emotions.

Green robots

New robots could help look after the environment. From recycling rubbish to protecting rare animals, and even eating pollution in the sea, they could work to protect the planet.

Nanorobots can be smaller than a blood cell.

Nanorobots

Scientists are trying to make robots that are too small to see. These "nanobots" could be used inside the body. Doctors could use them to hunt down germs or deliver medicines.

Robot facts and figures

Robots are amazing machines. Here are some weird and wonderful facts about robots that you can impress your friends with!

The word "**robot**" comes from the Czech word "**robota**", meaning **drudgery, or forced labour**. It was **first used** in a play in **1921**.

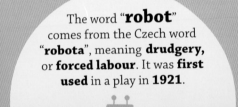

2040

It is thought that robots might become as clever as humans by 2040.

4,542

4,542 litres (1,200 gallons) per minute is the amount of water the firefighting robot Thermite 3.0 can spray to put out a fire.

Method V2 is a robotic suit with two legs controlled by a HUMAN PILOT.

TOPIO is a robot that **plays table tennis.**

A NANOBOT can be **less than one-thousandth** of a **millimeter**. That's even **smaller** than a **full stop**.

Hello!

Scientists have created a robot called CRAM that looks like a **GIANT COCKROACH**. It can squeeze through **small gaps** and could be used to find people trapped at a disaster site.

32

32 kph (20 mph) WildCat's top speed, making the fastest robot on legs – that isn't plugged in.

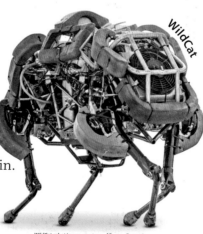

WildCat

WildCat robot image courtesy of Boston Dynamics

3,500

About 3,500 people from more than 40 countries take part in the annual football tournament RoboCup.

Glossary

Here are the meanings of some words that are useful for you to know when learning about robots.

3D printing Way to make a solid object using a printer. Most 3D printers squeeze liquid plastic out of a thin tube one layer at a time

actuator Part of a machine that makes it move, such as a motor

agricultural robot Robot that works on a farm

amphibian Cold-blooded animal that starts life in the water

android Robot that has a human face

animatronics Machines that look like real humans or animals. They are often used in films and theme parks

artificial intelligence When a machine can think for itself. Artificial intelligence can be shortened to "AI"

automaton Machine that repeats the same movements. Automata are often driven by water, air, or clockwork

autonomous Device that works on its own without human help

biomimetic Objects made by copying animals or plants

clockwork Machine that works using cogs and gears. It must be wound up to work

cobot Robot that works safely with human co-workers

code Written commands used in a computer program

computers Machines that can perform different tasks by following programs

console Device containing controls for a machine

domestic robot Robot made to work in the home

drone Flying machine with no pilot

electricity Type of energy that can be used to power machines

environment Area that someone lives in, or that a machine works in

factory Building where lots of the same objects are made

haptic When we feel objects through our sense of touch and body movement

humanoid Robot with a body shaped like a human. Humanoids usually have a head and arms, and often legs

industrial robot Robot that works in a factory

industry Business of making things in factories, such as cars

International Space Station Large space station and laboratory that orbits the Earth. It can be shortened to "ISS"

interstellar space Area of space between stars

joystick Small lever used to control a machine

machine Something that is powered by energy and is used to carry out a task

mechanical To do with machines, especially those with moving parts

microchip Tiny device that stores code in memory or runs programs

monitor Screen used for interacting with a computer

motor Device that changes electricity into movement. Motors are used to make robots move

nanotechnology Science that studies and makes tiny devices too small to see with the human eye

nursing robot Robot that helps to look after sick or injured people

power supply Source of energy that is used to make a machine work

probe Unmanned spacecraft designed to study objects in space and send information back to Earth

program Set of instructions a computer or robot follows to complete a task

programming Creating instructions for a robot to follow, written in a language that computers understand

programming language Set of words and rules used to give computers instructions

propeller Spinning blades used to push a machine or boat through water or air

prosthetic Artificial body part to replace one that is missing, such as a leg or hand

quadcopter Flying drone with four spinning helicopter blades

robot Moving machine that is programmed by a computer to do different tasks. They can sense their environment and respond

robotic Something that is, or is like, a robot

satellite Any object that travels around a planet, but often a manufactured machine that collects scientific information

sensor Part of an animal or machine that picks up information from its surroundings, such as eyes or a camera

sign language Way of talking using your hands. Different shapes are used for different letters and words

social robot Robot you can interact with. They can often talk and play

soft robot Robot made using soft, bendy materials rather than hard, rigid ones

surgery Operation on a patient to treat an injury or disease

swarm Collection of many animals or robots

technology Using scientific knowledge to create machinery and devices, such as robots

telepresence robot Robot with a screen that you can see and speak through. Usually used when you are in a different place to the robot

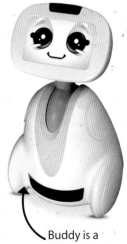

Buddy is a social robot.

Index

Acknowledgements

The publisher would like to thank the following people for their assistance in the preparation of this book: Fiona Macdonald and Rhea Gaughan for design assistance, and Garima Sharma for editorial assistance. Dan Crisp for illustrations; Polly Goodman for proofreading; Hilary Bird for compiling the index; and Dr Maja Matarić for her "Interview with…" interview.

The publisher would like to thank the following for their kind permission to reproduce their photographs:

(Key: a-above; b-below/bottom; c-centre; f-far; l-left; r-right; t-top)

1 UBTECH Inc.. 2 HANKOOK MIRAE TECHNOLOGY, www.k-technology.co.kr: (br). Harvard University: Lori Sanders (bc). 3 EPFL (Ecole polytechnique fédérale de Lausanne): Konstantinos Karakasiliotis & Robin Thandiackal, BioRob, EPFL, 2013 (bc). Festo AG & Co. KG: (tr). Getty Images: YOSHIKAZU TSUNO / AFP (br). Robotical Ltd.: (crb). University of Sydney and Australian Centre for Field Robotics: (c). Wonder Workshop: (bl). 4 Getty Images: TOSHIFUMI KITAMURA / AFP (ca, cr). NASA: JPL-Caltech / MSSS (c, cb). 4-5 Getty Images: PHILIPPE DESMAZES / AFP (ca). 5 From/by Softbank Robotics: (c, cb). Getty Images: PHILIPPE DESMAZES / AFP (ca). 6 Dorling Kindersley: Dave King / Science Museum, London (b). Rex Shutterstock: Everett Kennedy Brown / EPA (crb). The Metropolitan Museum of Art: Bequest of Cora Timken Burnett, 1956 (l). 7 Dorling Kindersley: Dave King / Rotring UK Ltd (br). Getty Images: Keystone-France (cl); Science & Society Picture Library (cra). Image courtesy of SRI International: (bc). 8 Geminoid™ HI-4: Osaka University: (c, clb). Getty Images: Noam Galai / Stringer (crb). Science Photo Library: Peter Menzel (br). 9 Alamy Stock Photo: ZUMA Press, Inc. (cra). Getty Images: Neilson Barnard (tc); Bloomberg (tr); Science & Society Picture Library (bl). Science Photo Library: Peter Menzel (clb); Sam Ogden (cla). UC Berkeley Engineering: (crb); F. Ofli, R. Chaudhry, G. Kurillo, R. Vidal, R. Bajcsy,"MHAD: A Comprehensive Multimodal Human Action Database", Workshop on the Applications of Computer Vision, pp. 53 - 60, 2013 (br). 10 Boston Dynamics: Atlas Robot image courtesy of Boston Dynamics (cla). HOOBOX Robotics: (cra, crb). 10-11 Dorling Kindersley: Merritt Cartography: Ed Merritt. 11 Alamy Stock Photo: Rodrigo Reyes Marin / AFLO (ca); CTK Photo / Radek Petrasek (cl). (c)RIKEN: (ca, cr). Panos Pictures: Tim Dirven (fcl). University of Sydney and Australian Centre for Field Robotics: (crb, bc). 12 Consequential Robotics / Eaglemoss: (bc). Nanda Home Inc.: (bl). Rethink Robotics: (cra). 13 Getty Images: Chris Rogers (tl). Intuitive Surgical, Inc.: (cla). Knightscope, Inc.: (cra). NASA: (cr, bl, br). 14-15 Alamy Stock Photo: Agencja Fotograficzna Caro. 15 Alamy Stock Photo: Kristoffer Tripplaar / Rethink Robotics (cb). 16 iRobot Corporation: (cb). Parrot SA: (tr). Blue Frog Robotics: (c). 16-17 Dorling Kindersley: Dan Crisp. 17 Moley Robotics: (cr). Nanda Home Inc.: (ca). Pal N Paul Inc.: (cr). 18-19 Intuitive Surgical, Inc.: © 2009 Intuitive Surgical, Inc. Used with permission.. 20 Alamy Stock Photo: WENN Ltd / BigDog robot image courtesy of Boston Dynamics (br); ZUMA Press, Inc. (clb). Getty Images: YOSHIKAZU TSUNO / AFP (cra). 21 Getty Images: Chris Rogers (tl). Knightscope, Inc.: (bl). NAVY.mil: (br). 22-23 Showbots Engineering GmbH: http://compressorhead.rocks: Joe Hency, New York City. 23 Consequential Robotics / Eaglemoss: (crb). Getty Images: Sean Gallup (cr). 24 NASA: (cra/Neptune); JPL (c, cra/Voyager); JPL-Caltech / MSSS (bc). 24-25 NASA: JPL-Caltech / 2MASS. 25 ESA: ESA, image

by C.Carreau (cr); Rosetta / NAVCAM (bl). NASA: (tc); NASA Johnson (tr); JPL / Cornell University (clb); JPL-Caltech / Space Science Institute (bc). 26 Alamy Stock Photo: Piero Cruciatti / Alamy Live News (br). Getty Images: Chris McGrath / Staff (bl). Waymo: (c). 27 Getty Images: YOSHIKAZU TSUNO / AFP (bl); John Phillips / Stringer (c). Piaggio Fast Forward: (tl, cra). Robotical Ltd.: (br). 28 Depositphotos Inc: prescott10 (clb). 28-29 www.poppy-project.org: (c). 29 www.poppy-project.org: (br). 30 UBTECH Inc.. 31 UBTECH Inc.: (cl, clb, bc). 32 Festo AG & Co. KG: (bl). iStockphoto.com: sirastock (fbl). 32-33 Wyss Institute at Harvard University: (c). 33 Harvard John A. Paulson School of Engineering and Applied Sciences: (r). 34-35 Getty Images: Barcroft Media. 35 Alamy Stock Photo: Sergio Azenha (br). Depositphotos Inc: pilipenkoD (cr). Getty Images: Barcroft Media (crb). 36 Korea Research Institute of Ships and Ocean Engineering: (c). NASA: Lora Koenig / NASA Goddard (cla). Teddy Seguin: Osada / Seguin / DRASSM (bc). 37 Alamy Stock Photo: Danita Delimont (br); REUTERS (c). NASA: NASA / JPL-CalTech (cra). 38 EPFL (Ecole polytechnique fédérale de Lausanne): Konstantinos Karakasiliotis & Robin Thandiackal, BioRob, EPFL, 2013 (l). University of Essex: Prof Huosheng HU (cr). 39 Festo AG & Co. KG: (tr, cra, bc). National Science Foundation, USA: Mark R. Cutkosky, Stanford University; Sangbae Kim, MIT (cla). Wyss Institute at Harvard University: (br, crb). 40-41 Dinomotion. 40 Dinomotion: (clb). 42-43 Harvard University: Leah Burrows (All Octobot Screengrabs). 43 Festo AG & Co. KG: (cra). 44 123RF.com: Nolre Lourens (cra). Dorling Kindersley: Lol Johnson Photography (c, crb, fcra, crb/Touch). 45 123RF.com: seamartini (cra). Getty Images: YOSHIKAZU TSUNO / AFP (bc); Tomohiro Ohsumi (cb/Nextage). Luke Cramphorn and Nathan Lepora, Tactile Robotics Group, Bristol Robotics Laboratory, University of Bristol: (cb). Mayfield Robotics: (cr). The University of Kassel: Prof. Dr.-Ing. Andreas Kroll (ca/RoboGasInspector). Willow Garage: (cla). 46 From/by Softbank Robotics: (cl, c, r). 47 © Engineered Arts Limited: (l). Getty Images: YOSHIKAZU TSUNO / AFP (cra). ©IIT – Istituto Italiano di Tecnologia: (c). UBTECH Inc.: (br). 48 Blue Frog Robotics: (bl). 49 Alamy Stock Photo: Science History Images (cra). From/by Softbank Robotics: (bc). Mayfield Robotics: (bl). 50 Getty Images: Bloomberg (cl). Rex Shutterstock: Eric Gay / AP (cra); Martin Cleaver / AP (cr). 51 Getty Images: John B. Carnett / Bonnier Corporation (cr); Koichi Kamoshida (clb). 52 Getty Images: KAZUHIRO NOGI / AFP (cl). Mayfield Robotics: (cr). 53 Getty Images: MARK RALSTON / AFP (cr); BSIP / UIG (cl). 54 Florence Hui. 55 Florence Hui: (clb, cra). 56 Construction Robotics: (tl). EPFL (Ecole polytechnique fédérale de Lausanne): Biorobotics Laboratory, EPFL (tr). Wonder Workshop: (c). 57 123RF.com: nobeastsofierce (bl). EPFL (Ecole polytechnique fédérale de Lausanne): Biorobotics Laboratory, EPFL (tr). Getty Images: Boston Globe (cb). RSE:RobotsISE.org: (cr). 58 HANKOOK MIRAE TECHNOLOGY, www.k-technology.co.kr: (r). Howe & Howe Technologies,Inc.: (br). 59 Boston Dynamics: WildCat robot image courtesy of Boston Dynamics (bl). Getty Images: VCG (br). TOSY Robotics Company: (tr). UC Berkeley Engineering: Courtesy of PolyPEDAL Lab, UC

Berkeley (cr). 60 Wonder Workshop: (tl). 61 Blue Frog Robotics: (br). 62 Mayfield Robotics: (tl). 64 Robotical Ltd.: (tl). 42-43 Harvard University: Lori Sanders (c).

Endpaper images: *Front:* Courtesy Stanford Special Collections and University Archives: cra (John McCarthy); Getty Images: Bettmann clb, Time Life Pictures / Mansell / The LIFE Picture Collection bl, DEA PICTURE LIBRARY cla (Sketch), Science & Society Picture Library cra (Unimate), crb (Cybernetic tortoise), Image courtesy of SRI International: br; *Back:* Getty Images: VCG tr (Right); Harvard University: Lori Sanders fcrb; ©IIT – Istituto Italiano di Tecnologia: cr iRobot Corporation: crb; Rethink Robotics: br (Right) Rex Shutterstock: clb (Zeus); Science Photo Library: Peter Menzel fclb, Sam Ogden bl; ©Sony Corporation: cla (ERS);

Cover images: *Front:* 123RF.com: Audrius Merfeldas bc; Depositphotos Inc: iLexx cla, pilipenkoD tr; Festo AG & Co. KG: crb; Getty Images: Peter Macdiarmid cra ©IIT – Istituto Italiano di Tecnologia: cr; Intuitive Surgical, Inc.: © 2009 Intuitive Surgical, Inc. Used with permission. fcr; NASA: l; Piaggio Fast Forward: crb/(Gita); Blue Frog Robotics: br; University of Sydney and Australian Centre for Field Robotics: cl; Wonder Workshop: c; Back: Alamy Stock Photo: Agencja Fotograficzna Caro crb; ESA: tr; Festo AG & Co. KG: cla NASA: bl; *Spine:* Wonder Workshop; *Front Flap:* Alamy Stock Photo: ZUMA Press, Inc. cl; (c)RIKEN: cr/ (Quiz Answers); EPFL (Ecole polytechnique fédérale de Lausanne): Konstantinos Karakasiliotis & Robin Thandiackal, BioRob, EPFL, 2013 ca; Festo AG & Co. KG c; From/by Softbank Robotics: clb/ (Quiz Answers); Getty Images: YOSHIKAZU TSUNO / AFP fcl, Sean Gallup bc; ©IIT – Istituto Italiano di Tecnologia: br/ (Quiz Answers); Knightscope, Inc.: cla/ (Quiz Answers) Korea Research Institute of Ships and Ocean Engineering: cb; Nanda Home Inc.: crb/ (Clocky); NASA: tr/ (Quiz Answers), STS-129 Crew, Expedition 2 Crew, NASA cra; Pal N Paul Inc.: cla; Rethink Robotics clb; UBTECH Inc.: br; Wonder Workshop: cra/ (Dash and Dot); Wyss Institute at Harvard University: cr; *Back Flap:* NASA: crb

All other images © Dorling Kindersley
For further information see:
www.dkimages.com

My Findout facts:

Timeline of robotics

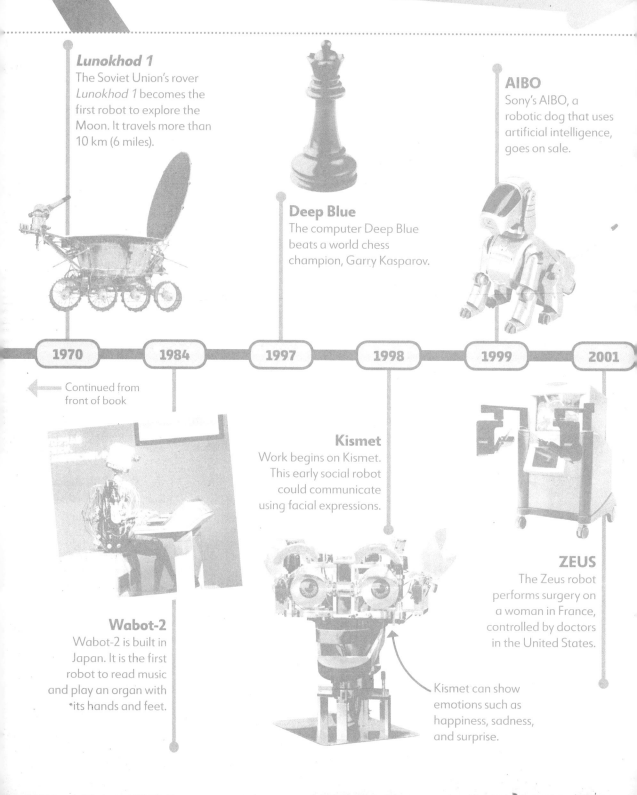

Lunokhod 1
The Soviet Union's rover *Lunokhod 1* becomes the first robot to explore the Moon. It travels more than 10 km (6 miles).

Deep Blue
The computer Deep Blue beats a world chess champion, Garry Kasparov.

AIBO
Sony's AIBO, a robotic dog that uses artificial intelligence, goes on sale.

1970 **1984** **1997** **1998** **1999** **2001**

Continued from front of book

Kismet
Work begins on Kismet. This early social robot could communicate using facial expressions.

Wabot-2
Wabot-2 is built in Japan. It is the first robot to read music and play an organ with its hands and feet.

ZEUS
The Zeus robot performs surgery on a woman in France, controlled by doctors in the United States.

Kismet can show emotions such as happiness, sadness, and surprise.